MW01013917

# Serious Pink

# Serious Pink

EKPHRASTIC POEMS

## Sharon Dolin

MARSH HAWK PRESS / 2003

FIRST EDITION

03 04 05 7 6 5 4 3 2 1

Marsh Hawk Press books are published by Poetry Mailing List, Inc., a not-for-profit coporporation under United States Internal Revenue Code.

Cover painting: *Sad Flowers* by Howard Hodgkin.
Used by permission of the Anthony d'Offay Gallery, London
Author photo: Alfredo Rossi
Book design: Claudia Carlson

Printed in the United States by McNaughton & Gunn

Library of Congress Cataloging-in-Publication Data

Dolin, Sharon.
    Serious pink / by Sharon Dolin.
        p. cm.
    ISBN 0-9713332-6-2
    1. Painting–Poetry. I. Title.
    PS3554.O438 S47 2003
    811'.54–dc21
                                    2002153581

MARSH HAWK PRESS
PO Box 220, Stuyvesant Station
New York, NY 10009
www.marshhawkpress.org

ACKNOWLEDGMENTS

Grateful acknowledgment is made to the following publications where these poems, occasionally in earlier drafts, have appeared:

*American Letters & Commentary*: "Sirens," "Day Dreams"
*American Literary Review*: "Discarded Clothes"
*Cimarron Review*: "Street"
*Crania* (internet): "The Moon"
*CrossConnect* (internet and print annual): "Objects," "Black Painting #8: Predicament"
*Drunken Boat* (internet): "Ode to Color"
*Ekphrasis*: "Black Painting #7: Metamorphosis"
*ForPoetry.com* (internet): "Sad Flowers"
*The Iowa Review*: "In the Honeymoon Suite"
*Jacket* (internet): "Fruit"
*The Journal*: "Black Painting #2: The Dead," "Black Painting #4: Bullfight"
*Lingo*: "After Dinner," "Love Letter"
*Orpheus Grid*: "Sea-Wall," "Prayer"
*Pequod*: "Jealousy," "Lovers"
*Poetry Flash*: "Black Painting #1: 'No Black'"
*PoetryMagazine.com* (internet): "Mistakes," "Ocean Park No. 64," "Black Painting #4: Bullfight," "Day Dreams"
*Poetry New York*: "Seated Woman," "Ocean Park No. 43"
*Salonika*: "Cerulean Interlude," "Black Painting #9: Betrayal," "Black Painting #10: Swivel," "Out of Sequence," "In the Black Kitchen," "Writing ~~Painting~~: A Ghazal," "Gossip"
*6ix*: "Black Painting #5: Twister," "Black Painting #11: Duel"
*So to Speak*: "Black Painting #13: Triptych"
*The Yalobusha Review*: "A Small Thing"

Section I was published in 1999 as a limited-edition chapbook under the title *Mistakes* in the *Poetry New York Pamphlet Series* (Vol. 24, 1999).

"Day Dreams" was printed as a letterpress broadside (The Center for Book Arts, 2002).

"It Started With a Woman" was exhibited alongside Joy Walker's paintings in *Women Artists Series: 1998–1999*, a group show held at Rutgers University Mabel Smith Douglass Library, and was printed in the catalogue.

"Writing ~~Painting~~: A Ghazal" appeared in the anthology *Ravishing Disunities: Real Ghazals in English*, edited by Agha Shahid Ali (Wesleyan University Press, 2000).

"Jealousy" appeared in the anthology *The Poets' Grimm: 20th Century Poems from Grimm Fairy Tales*, edited by Jeanne Marie Beaumont and Claudia Carlson (Story Line Press, 2003).

My gratitude to Phillis Levin, Jeff Friedman, Ellen Geist, Rachel Wetzsteon, Alfredo Rossi, Patricia Carlin, Rachel Weintraub, Cassandra Garbus, and Amy Lipman for their unstinting friendship and support. Thanks also to the editors of Marsh Hawk Press.

I would like to thank Yaddo and The Virginia Center for the Creative Arts where some of these poems were first written or revised.

*For Barry*

*I long to make pictures that will speak for themselves . . .*
—HOWARD HODGKIN

# CONTENTS

## I / Mistakes

## II / My Black Paintings

# III / Ode to Color


# IV / Serious Pink

# I / Mistakes

*Everyone makes mistakes. I'm a little ashamed of them in my pictures, so I obliterate them. You can't see what I consider mistake in my work. . .*

— RICHARD DIEBENKORN

# It Started With a Woman

and three coffee cups.
She was reaching for one of them
or else setting them down, one by one
this one on a stack of books and then that one
until peacock blue intervened
and all I could think about were the birds—
one red songbird on our windowsill
a visitation—an annunciation, really—
and what was it announcing with its complex fruity song:
its migratory loves, our ecstatic leap
into spring, its peerless whistling at the sky bluing up
every morning earlier and earlier so you almost feel
who needs coffee with this song and brilliant sky and the air
even though it's filled with jackhammers and trucks retarring Broadway
and the woman's head fills a window of even deeper blue—and over
a robin's egg blue window the song trills on

# Ocean Park No. 64

*after Buson*

Look closely at the under-drawing
stallion         you rode off in a blur         underwater

—corralled by luminous white-washed blue
fencing of the earliest dawn sky: *The short night—*

*near the pillow*
*a screen turning silver*

Memory is a fever-trapeze of lines resolving into images
              underpainted by association.

What if he simply tore down the building and left the scaffolding—

# Seated Woman

Say you're drawn to figure
      the anchored curvature
           of wet arms blurry
averted stares
      into saucerless cups
           of black coffee.

You'll find the difference between posing and life is

           Fingers over her eye—how long?
           Her slouch is not saucy, tell her
           to read the front page then
           read the front page.

You'll find the difference between line and color is

Words want to be story
      or song, raise the cup
           to narrative, then break it

           round pitchers shadows
           profile of breast and head
           bowed into afternoon.

With an arm along the table
      gather the bright wheaten light
      into the cradle of an arm:

knuckles induce
      crabby amusement
           over smudgy knees

           vertical stripes
           cascading down a
           sleeveless blouse.

## Sea-Wall

Randomness is the opposite of being adored.

Where there is minute definition color concentrates.

Gash of green before the slip
down to sea                    where a couple embraces.

Tired of branches overhead sectors
of land                         organize sky from leftover sea
and a pier they've strolled onto.

The sea made of segments of indeterminate
color this way of proceeding
                            might interest you
if you didn't want to go somewhere
and arrive or at least get closer.

This anxious waiting for progress
only witnessed
as having happened after all
                        on closer inspection
the couple appears
to be nothing but arcs of a
                        red isthmus — now we're
getting somewhere now we've slipped.

## Mistake

Mistakes are what you leave out
for other people to put away.

They are the picture painted out of
the picture which is nonsense
because already I can picture them.

Mistakes are the only thing you can trust
to go wrong and that's how
they right themselves no matter how
much you knock them over.

From the outside it might be a blemish
or stumble; inside it's the scar
of who you are.

The point of interest in any story
is where it goes off the tracks.

That's how we keep track of time
or time keeps track of us.

If it all came out right the first time
I'd be an automatic writer
and I'm not.

But this is coming out all right, isn't it?

# Looking Again

Say she's posed in a random gesture
of elbows crowning her head
her upper arm slopes down
above her breasts (in the next chair
the almost invisible cat). To see beforehand
or know before saying was never my forté
—nor his judging from the black wall entering this studio
in a rumble of uncertainties.
After looking again let's say she's unclasping
a necklace or tying a bit of blue around
her neck that flew up from the canvas back
of the director's chair. Shoes left on a patterned tile—
It's not true you never have to travel;
her knee's been cooked so long in his
attention it's burnt red as is the spot
between her breasts so fiercely shadowed
we look away to look back.

# Sirens

Uncountable, jutting out thin breasts and wailing

All torso, stiff and leaning gray mottled skin the texture of wet newspaper

| If this | then | sweeping |
| is not | to arrest | lemon |
| the way | your | hair |
| to make | attention | pink |
| friends | pale | shoulders |

No rocks to dash against just this rusty border of trees

Part the curtains *Who who who*
*will wait for us. . . . When when will you*
*come again. . . .* unplayed flutes lean off the ledge

      Peacock blue will cool your eyes
    get you out of the boat climb
the cliff-face and join us

       We'll smooth your hair and sing
     with such dazzlement
   we'll even part company—the tines
of a fork splitting off

And you're captivated again by the image

# Objects

Enter the saucer
coiled of air

       murky clouds on the table
       rainswept into a spiral

cup of dark water
there are enough

       frangible moments to
       make this an ars

poetica of form
lanced of content:

       poppies may be as orange
       as the line

down the table's center
which does not go

       with the shadow
       is blue.

The album opened
onto a room a letter

       that was never forgiven
       coffee mug pools in shadow.

If I could tell you
without anxious precision

       mistrals of feeling
       I would not have to

skip around so.

# Street

This is the city
alleyway of windows
with shadows passing for time:

if it ends in an ocean or river of inanition
those roofs of powder blue and
terracotta pink could be a childhood sky

could be trees fusing
into a grand piano
of kelly green

could be sheets of apricot rain
on mountains passing their shadows
off as clouds

and there you are in the rearview
cut out and refracted onto the road

among silent palms
uniform slope of stucco beneath
a whitened density of blue

so that houses seem carved
from a topiary of air and earth

as your eyes rove over hills
in an atavistic search
for the sea.

# Ocean Park No. 43

Several random rooftops protrude—
          middleground pentimenti of lavender-eggwhite
             density. Hunt terns on the pool's
               perimeter? These are city walls, after all,
          these buildings have levels—not quite rectangular
nor triangular, what were you expecting?

Pentimenti aren't mis-steps but reflections
        building up in the pond you're rowing in—which is nothing
           compared to aquamarine pools of L.A.
           where a lipstick left open melts
        into an ars rosetica. Elsewhere, stepladder
grids bracket the back of black.

Against the purity of a white wall
dancers' curves harden in plaster.

# Ochre

Whatever was first there
    may continue to exist
        you can still make out

        fugitive pinks and blues
    saved by white
diagonal

and the stucco house with trellis
    trailing woodbine
        until midsummer glare intervenes.

        I've given you two ideas:
    forethought and afterthought
overlaid by a Venetian-green door.

You are mistaken if you think I planned it this way

only by being mistaken
    about diagonal rose
        beside powder blue

could I hope to swathe almost all in honey

live life not as one grand mistake
    but as shards of thousands
        with time to cover the bruise

        play with the watermark
    pull down an ochre shade
and let the shapes—once removed—

move you.

# Berkeley Numbers

1.

Pretty strong stuff this time of forgiveness
    when sun bleaches memory of shade.
Just do one thing then the next and hope
    one gets canceled out or obscured
as afternoon shade does the figure.

Imagine walking with an aerial view
    filled with dreams of escape
from suburban round of bicycle and
    espresso grounds. Dreams of a city
never found.

2.

If you put mauve and pink feathers
    cool purples of the jacaranda together
you have a patch of working color
    of impossible abstract afternoons by the pool
eucalyptus cooling your lungs.

3.

I wouldn't have written except you asked:
these planted things scumble the view.

4.

Muddy as memory
    of some three-night sincerity
dark field against the light:
    found on a rainy night in a Castro diner
open all hours to the working blind.
    Walked home to Cumberland Street

with two tongues as velvet as drink
       so that lying on top or beneath
felt like sleep.

5.

The bay returned to—
       scrannel memory
does nobody any good

awaken to schists of russet-apricot-flamingo

singing out
as the birds did all last night.

# Prayer

Everybody likes lines, how come
            they make you so uneasy
look for fundamental disarray
or what's been gone over?
            This life sure hasn't, else how'd you blow
so many chances to picture—
                        pictures to chance?

        (Remember you awoke in the middle of the night
        prayed then forgot when your prayer was answered.)

It's all in the wrist and shadows
or ghosts of who you thought you were
                        emerge even as you deny them.

            Someday they'll let us speak
            our amber resonances and be done.
                        We thought we knew we didn't know.
            Never free of gauze        over gaze

            or the years-ago face left behind
            the yellow house you drew as a child—
            your first floating house waiting to be    unseen again.

Charcoal-gray bands sweep silver blue
triangular
        rust by angular storm clouds.

Compared to line shaped color is anodyne
                        until the ghosts return
you to the cups—only now

There's one and some oranges
or just rind and soda bottle
                    peacock-blue tablecloth striped
the shape of your beloved's shirt.

The bird has been swallowed
by evening though his red feathers
                    stained our floor with song.

# Ocean Park No. 79

Periwinkle drowns pentimenti—almost
could be a headline

stacking blocks in the corner by the powerlines

Every blue          a pool          for diving in

though tomato red spikes through
so busy the eye          jumps / settles
on canary yellow—not entirely—smudged out.

Possible to make an art of imperfect accident?

Call them *riflessioni*:
Mistakes submerged—admired as underwater plants or bottom-
                                        feeding fluke.

# Ocean Park No. 45

*When I arrive at the idea,*
*the picture is done,* said Diebenkorn,

but what if color is so saturated
with arrivals it undoes doing—

ideas—completions—ice-blue
panels cooling our forehead. No coincidence

is replicable when the idea is a closed
line I cross the border

into (you have no idea, that's the idea)
an early spring field of young grass blades

the line between being green
and seeming green

is a line—there stands
a whitewashed barn

of sun-bleached planks leading to a song
(is color idea or means—or ideal means)

of buttercups ruled out
despite this departure

into frank curvature of flowers.

# Ocean Park No. 96

The painter called his "crudities"
uncertain stumblings others call
                    regrets
            and tuck away.
        Here they take on
    diagonal pallor, sand-gray beach
when umbrellas have all been folded and
terns and gulls score over the human surface
buff surf or could be "grain stacked in the
shape of a house" (*Diebenkorn* in old Swedish)
in one corner midnight-blue buoy so you don't sink
orange opaque slab and the sky—a lesser feature—
    however much eyes always tend to look up.

# II / My Black Paintings

*My black paintings—although there's no black in any of them.*

—JOAN MITCHELL

# Black Painting #1: "No Black"

"No black" except
this encroaching

difficulty: disturbed
profile

shaped clots
in the thicket of hair

urged toward avian forms

buildup
toward opacity

gives way to flight
of Chinese calligraphy

resisting static shape
pigment

over pigment
dark flurry

if you look
if you insist

# Black Painting #2: The Dead

Blue winter rain
that's what you've become

cloud
whitewashed by weather

this window
beyond being

the elements eat you

damp cold
of the first winter

now the second
you said you wanted

to travel
now you're still

blotches of flight
descend into your

stationary car

# Black Painting #3: Turning

Not sheer
vertical
scree marks
of rain
nor splotches
of growth along
the coast—
life is sometimes
nothing
but figure /
ground
reversals:
figure
turning into
ground
turning, just
turning
constant
knell
to wake up
fresh-fleshed
percipient
green
against—
the more one looks—
miraculous white
holds Chinese
characters in palimpsest
blue and yes
even green

# Black Painting #4: Bullfight

It could have been a bullfight
who knows which way we were running
it came after us

(the blurry clown could not hold
anyone's attention)

the horse     ridden in     the picador
was gored—who?
yes, arched his back
wasn't it what we all desired

passional thrust
when the bull pierces
your thigh

but what is a nun doing on horseback?

# Train Interlude

As on
the train
where he
always
sketches
someone asleep
because
then finally
we are our
singular selves
unencumbered
by glance
or self-regard

As at the end
of love-
making I
say you
are my other
half and you
only half-
wince at
such stark
platonism

But what is
miraculous
in bed
when air
gets closest
to liquid

we are
all knees
hard to tell
whose are
whose

# Black Painting #5: Twister

Now it's finally condensing
    that core of darkness
        at the center of any
day—especially in rain
        especially when green
            birds tinge
            the edges
    with brooding
    strokes quick
    tails of blue knock
    at the dark scratch-
    marks against white surely
    only such whiteness blue
    fury mixed with reddish
    green forgetting could
    make a dark well
    to plummet all
    irretrievable
    losses

# Black Painting #6: Clouds

A cloud with legs!
Who would have ridden
or carried it

to where I sit
and for the moment
no one else is shaded

or else everything is
cloud-cover: miraculous
powdered wisps

and whoever rides
beneath is caught
in some infernal shadow

inkblot of loss
that keeps running forward—
shadowy scythe

cutting through
relentless buffoonery
of white

# Black Painting #7: Metamorphosis


Turn your body into
      a vase of patches
           and strokes

become a patchwork of gestures

you're playing on the diagonal now
      having scotched all other positions
           the bow sweeps across your neck and shoulders

until you're a tube of tears squeezed
into the next moment

who ever supposed pain
      would make a monument of shaped
           density

      nothing has crystallized
      either the white wave has
      covered too much or receded
      in its fullness

      you're a green body of notes
sprung from a red-and-blue cocoon

# Black Painting #8: Predicament

*Portrait of Joan Mitchell*


It's the same predicament:
what to start with, what to fix
on—causes or results,
feelings or the outer effects

this was a way of knowing
this ecstatic embrace
this yes to windy clouds
passing a skyscape
where land had been obliterated

could be a continent forming
could be chicken scratch
is just chicken scratch

there is no original whiteness
only spaces being filled up
then blocked out

so if she keeps going
past the white cigarette
past the favorite part of day
when attention has already slid
into a contemplative pool

then the application of this red
now this blue then an olive region

until the eye refreshes itself
as at dusk when colors become
showy flowers before closing
themselves into shade

now it has passed—
and the way shifts
to an impermanent yellow of what ifs
and can I

a retreat moving toward
the center and its perimeter
each one indistinguishable

try drawing a reflection
with a stick that has
agitated the surface
into a giddy muddle
just beginning to settle

# Cerulean Interlude

After a long time adrift

comes a reappraisal
a trophy of obstinacy

or call it the shaped mind
stampeding into white

after pain passes
we're dumbstruck

by winter blue
that doesn't admit any haze

by welcoming arms
laughing grin

whatever remains

# Black Painting #9: Betrayal

Almost eighteen months        unimaginably quiet

life's betrayal        such whiteness

added to        blue attention

always there arises some        splaying toward

inattentiveness        amid so much loss and saying

unsay for a while        take back the rampant reds

carve a Medusa in profile        obliterate all full-faced wishes

# Black Painting #10: Swivel


In the midst of gray this
robust
        swivel
of patched light
called morning

his heart        his heart

assignation of flowers

the chair rolls back
underneath
there's a floor
underneath
a sigh

# Black Painting #11: Duel

Attracted
to repulsion
a couple

of arms flurry
behind hot-sauce
windows

blue cap
-sizing
red

all mirrors
are deadly
because they ask

which one
which one is
you

above smoke
blue
raised brows

# Black Painting #12: Doubt

I don't know what you're expecting
except rain
and the monkey-web
of doubt

amid
dark green cloud
light
and a loud longing for spring's
invisible shoots

not knowing when
the cluster will fling
droplets
and if you will remain
until the last stroke

# Out of Sequence

This window we stare out of

bright basket
we dip into

until we're lowered
into a nightly cavern

of old stories mixing
with new faces gesturing

against the blind wall

habit is a hard shell
to shed

tears
luxuriant

# Black Painting #13: Triptych

Rest your eyes upon
abundant rain
about to fall—spring
in its immanent cloud-cover
I like you better this way
without that razzle-dazzle
shining glare splatter, knick-knack-
atory streets peeled open—a too-ripe banana

    The dancer on horseback listens to the four
    o'clock hour being struck
    reassured all these brushstrokes
    will amount to something
    a hand keeps lifting and dropping:
    does it know when to stop?

        A pause is a bird on one foot waiting
        for a call in response to its call
        from among all the others and the traffic
        even in Brooklyn new bird songs
        delicate white and pink buds
        for those who can stop green
        bushy outgrowths green-
        green as the lily ponds in Monet's garden

# Absence-Memory

Another window onto
aftereffects
of loss
speeding into
readiness
to plunge
again

into anger
circumvented by
frenetic strokes
and spikes

we didn't concern
ourselves with what
she meant
only with morning
light on the primed
branch

water travels
through landscape
searching
for some means of escape

ignorance being the
obverse of mystery

sometimes with greater
shapeliness

though still play-
fully irregular

# III / Ode to Color

# Ode to Color

A man in a red GEORGIA baseball cap wearing
        a sweatshirt with a red bulldog over his heart
        sitting in a subway car, the smell of his poverty much too strong

but I stay out of weakness and pity:
        his dark skin has gone through fire
        and his hands and arms and who knows how much more of him

wear the ropy scars: I watch him not wanting to stare
        as he draws out of a pocket dangling from a long rope at his waist
        a red-plastic compact that he opens:

the mercury pool he dips and dips his face towards
        as though to stanch the fire (who knows what he sees)
        he shuts it opens it shuts it then like a black Narcissus he has to re-open

and stares. Maybe it solidifies him, all I know is steeped
        in my own pool I keep seeing this portrait in red.

Δ

What's he trying to say
        with *Red on Maroon* or
        *Purple, White and Red*?

Has Rothko taken away
        saying, *pulverized*
        *the identity of things* so we lean

back on an imaginary grassy mat
        gazing at these stacked heavens—
        or has he broken in on our silence

so you and I can breathe and stretch
        our arms again?

Δ

Push the button on Cornell's *Lighted Dancer* she glows cobalt blue.

Red Sea Bird wrasse is long-nosed and blue

Δ

Spend your life inside
window's *wind-eye*

framed by goldenrod
gazing at exhalations of sky.

Rosettes
are not poppies
but moments of attention
burned into the wall.

Δ

*God's essence would ensure his existence.*
*Can one also say the essence*
*of color ensures its existence?*

> *What color is God.*
> *God's the color of water.*

Δ

Basket lady
semi-toothless
yodelled so sweetly

I wished the earplugs
from my ears and tossed
some change in
insisted I pick a bunch
of her flowers crudely
rubber-banded *Yes,*
*I like that one too*
blood-red rose and two pale lilac
roses I'd never seen that hue
before never seen a self
so abandoned to goodness
before

Δ

*A color will carry you*
*around the world immediately*

*Why this poverty when we deal with colors? Why comparisons?*
*Birch leaves are like small, pale-yellow coins, sparsely attached to twigs*
*which are of what hue? Lilac, from the lilacs, and violet, from the violet.*

Red as the blonde-bearded face
        bloodied by another fighting
        over deposit cans

or as miscarried week-old life
        draining out a full week
        between my legs.

Δ

What does reddish green or bluish orange or yellowish black look like?

*Black is not enough to show the absence of light.*

What if colors at night
　　　　look the way they do
　　to the colorblind in daylight?

Δ

When you take me against the rock

still pool sizzled to buttery glare
while others leap from cliffs

in green frolic where shoal
almost hardens to field—stripped

into memory
what will we become?

blue-toned stripes behind
the lime-green bar being brushed

by a wet black feather.

Δ

*What color do you like best, Tatu?*
*Black, black!*
*And you, Washoe. What color?*
*Red, red!*
*Why?*
*Beautiful, beautiful!*

Δ

*Think of a bluish orange, a reddish green, or a yellowish violet,*
*the same feeling as in the case of a southwesterly north wind.*

Δ

I envy the cuttlefish and squid; wish I could *think* color—
become any mottled hue into which I sink for cover.

Δ

What color is *The Barber of Seville?*
Teal-gray and teak (or bamboo)
with no trace of red or black.
Umbria is ochre and rust
dark brown as the centers of sunflowers
keening in late-summer sun.
Bologna is always foggy gray.
And Rome? Goldenrod.
And Paris? Peacock blue and gray.
Nantucket? Gray and more gray-blue studded
with Black-eyed-Susan yellow.
What about Tokyo? New York?
Which city is tomato-red? Mexico City.
But you've never been.
That doesn't matter.

Δ

*I like the color of your coat.*
*It's brown.*
*I wouldn't call it brown.*
Call it the color of bark, call it
the impasse of color.

Δ

Knobbed whelk on the beach
whose insides caught the light
bright orange twilight
siren song we had to approach.
—*There must be mussel inside*
—*It's just the shell color made stronger by the bending of the light*
A color so pearly rich our footsteps swung
toward it as toward the setting sun's mirror.

Δ

Diamondback rattler had colors impossible to recall or name:
snake-color will have to do. Maybe fear blanches things
of color and mystery bloods them—the fuzzy fruited
heart of the sago palm lint-covered ribs pulled back
and there the small smooth rosy heartbeats lay.

Δ

Go into the closet or bathroom
with these mushrooms and wait
longer than you think and then
their crowns will glow from underneath
sample these chicken o' the woods
the mycologist climbed trees to pick
more yellow than orange and edible
walk along the beach late afternoon
find two halves of an Eastern cockle
still joined splayed open rust-to-rose
their own internal sunset.

Δ

*Ancient idea that colour is afterthought.*

*Often when I settle down to work I begin by noting*

*the icy clearness of the sour blue sky.*

*You cannot approach color as if coming in a barn door.*

Δ

Her molten hair beside the stone-gray caviar

light has tigered its way into a figure
        black sofa speckled red with people eating

as flecks of words glint and rise
        in an evening sky until they fuse:
                vermilion—gold—blue.

Δ

*Vermilion cannot do everything*
Matisse enjoyed saying,
but had he seen the virgin's vermilion gown
with puffed mandarin-orange upper sleeves
tapered to violet-blue satin at the wrists
and the startled Mary from Recanati
holding her hands at chest height
from the force of unclasping them from prayer
ready to push away air of the intruder?

Whatever else Lotto meant I know he meant that red
as did Frederic Leighton for the sleeping *Flaming June*
a color so stunning it goes
by many names: cinnabar red, scarlet, China
red and calypso. Even God, so this story goes—
as though the angel clothed in pastel blue
holding a stalk of lilies would pale at the task—
flew down wearing the same
shocking vermilion cinched by cornflower blue
and reached into her room.
And I could spend an afternoon worshiping
at the foot of such rich hues
and did.

Δ

*When we are bathed in what radiates*
*we forget everything that borders on yellow or blue.*
*We imagine an absolutely pure red,*
*fine carmine suffered to dry on white porcelain.*

White to ward off
                    *the distracting din of colors*

Δ

Today all the colors have been mixed together.
*No harmony, the result is gray,* as Goethe knew
and the sky storing up its first snow contains them all.

                    *If I say a piece of paper is pure white and if snow*
                    *were placed next to it*
                    *and it then appeared gray . . .*

*Lemon-yellow-black was my idea of the underwing of the grasshopper*
*but the carmine in connection with the sunset is better.*

Δ

*Who shouted with glee*
*when the color blue was born?*

Lapis lazuli ground up as paint once more precious than gold—

gold the color a Jew was made to wear in the Middle Ages, a mark of shame
        until Michelangelo on the highest reach of wall beneath the ceiling

of the Cappella Sistina painted Moses in flowing robes of yellow
        painted Abraham Isaac Sarah all all in golden yellow.

Yellow for Goethe *the color nearest the light.*

*Blue still brings a principle of darkness with it*
        (to be blue) *an affinity with black*
        a brooding Northern blue

for Goethe even Roman blue
        best seen in full moonlight
        (*plenilunio*)

*This placid space . . .*
        *not so blue as we thought. To be blue,*
        *There must be no questions.*

*La terre est bleue comme une orange*
        the earth not really blue though round as?
        though in shadow in the bowl the orange may turn blue.

*There should be*
*so much more, not of orange, of*
*words, of how terrible orange is*
*and life.*

Enter my blood-orange frame
      letting cobalt waves
      wash over you—give way

      to pleasure then
      give it away.

What color is the universe?
      *Between aquamarine*
      *and turquoise.*

When asked his favorite color he
      blurted out blue (as his shirt)
      hers, like Lorca's, will always be green    green.

# I V / Serious Pink

*Can you imagine a serious pink next to a trivial blue or even a ridiculous black?*

— HOWARD HODGKIN

# Day Dreams

Let spectacled be speckled
and strips become tipples of stripes.

A wavery view loves a vapory hue,
an undulant curve, a redolent verve.

A donging clock polka-dots time,
does a stippled back chime?

At center is an ocean obscured by raging light

Serious pink seems to lean on everything
in spite of trivial blue candy canes—
curtain folds on a proscenium stage.

It all comes down to land scaping a backdrop
for other protagonal forms
(and the surround not always round)

And what you think they're doing, anyway,
humping or huddled there together on that beach
of light and black almost never out of reach.

# After Dinner

Set the just-to-be-eaten
    on a tray
    of blue flames

and cranberry shrubs
    blur gray
    under duck sauce.

Of course you prefer avocado,
    fish roe on black bread—
    what you see is what you remember

and what you remember is what's
    framed. Over blue-stemmed
    glasses of the driest sherry

Look, poppies sprung
    from the dung-heap center
    and cherries.

# Jealousy

Squares of burning sienna guard
an inner courtyard of lettuces

> moving you toward and away
> from a heart of burning reticence
> that soon became a mode of self—
> a defining mood of petulance.

To break the spell
> peer down
> the round-by-round
> stairwell

until you get so dizzy you see
these walls you've built, your russet ire
*let down, Rapunzel, let down,*
is the wood that stokes

her golden-haired fire.

# The Moon

Let me finally tell you what I'm made of:
      cork of icy trees

hewn from the inconstancies of your eye
      that blinks me oval, then cuticle.

All the dreams you refused
      or woke from—flown with gravity

to my dark side to seethe. I'm the cruise
      up the Nile you never took, the men

on street corners you grazed with your looks
      before you moon at me. If I have seas

they're made of lovers' tears
      and a few lunatics' too. I'm so cold I burn

so lonely I spurn and flee to my mountains
      while green flames from your atmosphere

lick my edges. I would be done with all of you.

# In the Honeymoon Suite

To go so inside
each person had to be mastered:

*they* scorned,
*he* and *she* banished

so that you and I
could reverse

up with down
then vanish.

All conversation is round

—sharp edges flung behind drapes
of red ochre streetlights.

        Inner cerise
        wet powder-green chemise.

    Cancans of blue thigh ride a risky elbow

Here figure is the ground upon which, sweet, we figure.

# A Small Thing

one sundazzled blue tulip
stemless almost without
separate petals but not shape-
less if you look carefully paired
with its orange shadow (in the dis-
tance chin-high swaying grasses)
the one you picked and held
before your face for hours
in speechless wonder gigantic
flowerhead of childhood:
the summer your body glowed
with sky and field and mossy pond
        it floated in

until you hardly notice the blackened edge
stippled pink          until you do

# Sad Flowers

Because their brilliance is so redundant
      yet redemptive.

Because we come to them with doubts
      about the beautiful almost religious.

Because the names we have given them—
      Indian Paintbrush, Owl Clover,
      Yellow Adder's-tongue, Goat's Rue,
      Prairie-Thistle, Scarlet Monkey-flower,
      Prairie Beard-tongue—upstage them.

Because a memory swiped from the Bay of Naples outlasts them.

Because they heal as they die.

Because we insist we prefer their steady colors
      when our heads turn at a mere squiggle
      or waver or smudge or ripple or splotch.

# Down in the Valley

Who doesn't love an aerial view:
the music of the field beside
the river's purple arc

we float above. Look, cabbages
the size of silos and radishes
unearthed for miles. The tree

in Eden gave us the will to soar
into a band of light and see
the world God made.

And though we're *rich and wearie*
we never need a rest from restlessness.
Seeing two or three smudges

of blue and green gives birth
to desire for the things of the world,
being mostly the desire to see them.

# Discarded Clothes

are flags of our own disapproval
lineaments of an evening we discard
as quickly as some friends.

If there's a freckled monument to gloom,
it passes. Lovers of the daily
who repeat for us an antic state

return with small remembrances of leaves.
We watch them buckle and heave, tell
of our quick departure into flesh

while lilies on the pond's edge
grow splotchy and dream:

*Your pants are made of wind,*
*your shirt from daisies blown*
*to dusty globes on the lake*
*by our breath.*

# Lovers

Brillantined hair in yoke-colored light
fathomed to a dizzy blur we reach
     and reach round for-
getting beginnings imply endings
we are suddenly all middle molten
kinesis spiked with a surety that doesn't
bother knowing its name if ecstasy
were a color this would be its bulls-
eye the place in the fire where glass
learns form from formlessness

and what are we but delight
coining each other's eyes
     a whirling
tunnel of startling
     entrances spun from light

# Love Letter

Ovals plant dark kisses, the mirror slants
to receive your goodness, your wishes.
Put in whatever you want: a stack of rare books,
how the room looks after you've closed your eyes—
if gloomier than expected, a glance
at how you look, by chance, alone.

      Ringed by a lapis pond, a stone
      continues to fall
      to recall you to the surface.

Scan your inner thigh       the death mask on the desk
then plunge into                     the surrounding
    ultramarine                       wave
        you                    make of me
      bamboo hill I           make of you.

# Fruit

Oh meteor of memory
most voluptuous apricot ever
        juice of you is a love letter
listing round my tongue you happened
        in a shuttered room in Tuscany
in a village so small we became local gossip
        so wet with you my tongue turned
into your fruit the sun burned down to a pit
        then the undulant hill swallowed it
male moose licks his lips to show he's
        ready what you showed me
that late afternoon in hot shadow
        was juice of apricot light
pouring over us into night

# In the Black Kitchen

Place yourself in a night
      field of giant colanders
            with holes so large

they let through everything—
      cabbages and what
            you wished you were doing

on that deck after all.
      Drink sweet vermouth
            then pour yourself around the couch.

The truffle hound's
      been rooting for a mate,
            the sauce must wait.

Here's a plate of moonlight
      topped with fireflies,
            huge lipstick smudge

on the patio glass
      (the tryst you missed)
            has saved many a guest's

forehead from a keen kitchen rapping.

# It Can't Be True

                what we heard about you
            how lopsided you've become
    fingerpainting your way

    out of that party, going blotto
            like a receding mirror
                    down a dizzy stairwell—who knew

    your thoughts grew excremental;
            in other views, a charming hue—
                    sea-blue became your motto

                    the splotchy frame your trademark.
            No wonder, being cooped up like that—
    the rank colors, the fumes have unhinged you.

    Rainmaker from inside
            a filthy windshield

                we wouldn't trust you to drive us anywhere.

# Writing ~~Painting~~: A Ghazal

*I go where it's blue.*
—William Gass


Splotches blotched among Prussian blue,
what words match red, wrong blue.

Peacock shimmy. Memory's sky.
Shapes insist: stories sung blue.

Choose everything: waterfall avenue;
cerulean roof drops flung blue.

Robin's eggs, unhatched, fly up;
orange drowns tongue blue.

Gone to pick berries. Be back
by two, hands stung blue.

Graze this shaggy bush for knowledge
of the good—having clung blue.

Irresistible—this erratic caress;
hair shaken wet, hung blue.

Past desert's edge—plum trees;
off the plain of Sharon—the sea rung blue.

# Gossip

*I heard what the talkers were talking,*
said Walt. And I haven't got a clue

who let them in here. What a way
to end: the blackened windowsill

we lean elbows on to watch the evening snow—
blotted out by angry words.

Why call it human to gab and blear
the face of memory with "news"?

Come look, the sky has moved
inside the window as if to call us back

to what's true (a banished view nowadays,
almost taboo). Yet still we go out for a stroll

pace the shore or prize a rooftop sunset
(amid the tinkling glasses, *He's shtupping someone*

*new—not you, dear*) the curving green light is our last view.

NOTES

Though all the poems in Sections I, II, and IV were written to be pictures that can speak for themselves, the three sequences are all ekphrastic: that is, the work of three different artists: Richard Diebenkorn, Joan Mitchell, and Howard Hodgkin informs them. For those interested in reading the poems beside their pictorial muses, the following notes are offered. Section III, "Ode to Color," borrows liberally with slight alterations from the thoughts of poets, painters, and philosophers on color.

**I:** Below are the individual poems' correspondences, where they exist, to paintings by Richard Diebenkorn, (all but one print) found in color reproductions in Gerald Nordland's *Richard Diebenkorn* (Rizzoli, 1987). Each of the numbered "Ocean Park" poems corresponds to the same-numbered *Ocean Park* painting.

"It Started with a Woman": *Girl and Three Coffee Cups*, 1957.

"Ocean Park No. 64": The verse translation of Buson's poem is from Robert
    Hass's *The Essential Haiku: Versions of Basho, Buson, & Issa* (Ecco
    Press).

"Seated Woman": *Woman at Table in Strong Light*, 1959 and *Woman with
    Newspaper*, 1960.

"Sea-Wall": *Seawall*, 1957.

"Looking Again": *Seated Nude—Black Background*, 1961.

"Sirens": *Ocean Park No. 6*, 1968.

"Objects": *Still Life with Letter*, 1961.

"Street": *Interior with View of Buildings*, 1962.

"Ochre": *Ochre*, 1983, color woodblock print, reprod. in *Richard
    Diebenkorn Prints:1948–1992* (Susan Sheehan Gallery, NY, 1993).

"Berkeley Numbers": based on Diebenkorn's "Berkeley" canvases, a
    numbered series of abstract landscapes, 1953–55.

"Prayer": *Ocean Park No. 24*, 1969 and *Still Life with Orange Peel*, 1955.

"Ocean Park No. 96": The Swedish derivation of Diebenkorn is in
    Nordland, Note 1.

**II:** This sequence is based on a series of paintings by Joan Mitchell that she painted in 1964 after the death of her father and when her mother was ill with cancer. They are darker than the characteristic Mitchell palette. She called them her "black paintings," though she claimed never to have used the color black in them. Similarly, the poems restrict the use of the word "black" to quoting Mitchell in the first poem. Each numbered poem corresponds to the painting with the same number, all reproduced in *Joan Mitchell: ". . . my black paintings . . ." 1964* (Robert Miller Gallery, 1994); the unnumbered titled poems, thought of as verbal interludes in the sequence, do not have pictorial correspondences.

**III:** "Ode to Color": Quotes from the following sources, sometimes edited or altered, in the order used:

Mark Rothko, as quoted in *Mark Rothko: A Biography*, by James E. B.
    Breslin (The University of Chicago Press).
Ludwig Wittgenstein, *Remarks on Colour*, trans. Linda L. McAlister &
    Margarete Schättle (University of California Press).
James McBride, *The Color of Water* (Riverhead Books).
Tomaz Salamun, from "King of Birds," *The Four Questions of Melancholy*
    (White Pine Press).
Czeslaw Milosz, "A Little Treatise on Colors," *Roadside Dog* (Farrar, Straus
    and Giroux).
A color manual for painters.
Two signing chimpanzees as quoted by Sarah Boxer, "It Seems Art Is
    Indeed Monkey Business," *The New York Times*, Nov. 8, 1997.
Roger Fry, "Plastic Colour," from *Transformations*, 1926.
Henri Matisse, "Notes of a Painter" (1908) in *Theories of Modern Art*, ed.
    Herschel B. Chipp (University of California Press).
Le Corbusier.

*Goethe's Theory of Colours* (1840), trans. Charles Lock Eastlake (MIT Press, 1970).

Marianne Moore, *The Selected Letters of Marianne Moore*, ed. Bonnie Costello (Alfred A. Knopf).

Pablo Neruda, *The Book of Questions*, trans. William O'Daly (Copper Canyon Press).

Wallace Stevens, "The Ultimate Poem Is Abstract."

Paul Eluard, "L'Amour, la Poésie."

Frank O'Hara, "Why I Am Not a Painter."

Neil deGrosse Tyson, "Colors of the Cosmos," in *Natural History*, March 2002.

**IV:** Each poem corresponds to a painting by Howard Hodgkin of the same or similar title (painted between 1976 and 1995), all found in color reproductions in *Howard Hodgkin Paintings* (Abrams, 1995).

"Down in the Valley": The epigraph and quoted phrase are from George Herbert's "The Pulley."

"Writing ~~Painting~~: A Ghazal": The epigraph is from William Gass's *On Being Blue* (David R. Godine).

ABOUT THE AUTHOR

Sharon Dolin is the author of a book of poems, *Heart Work*, (The Sheep Meadow Press, 1995), and four chapbooks: *The Seagull* (The Center for Book Arts, 2001); *Mistakes* (Poetry New York Pamphlet Series, 1999); *Climbing Mount Sinai* (Dim Gray Bar Press, 1996); and *Mind Lag* (Turtle Watch Press, 1982). Another collection of poems, *Realm of the Possible*, is forthcoming from Four Way Books in 2004. She has been the recipient of a national award from the Poetry Society of America, a Fulbright Scholarship to Italy, and has held several fellowships to Yaddo and The Virginia Center for the Creative Arts. Since 1995, she has been the Coordinator and Co-judge of the Center for Book Arts Annual Letterpress Poetry Chapbook Competition. She has taught at The Cooper Union, New York University, and The New School and currently teaches poetry workshops at The Unterberg Poetry Center of the 92nd Street Y in New York City, where she lives with her husband and young son.

## ABOUT THE BOOK


The text of this book was set in Electra. Designed in 1935 by William Addison Dwiggins, Electra has been a standard book typeface because of its even and legible design. Electra combines its classic roots with the Zeitgeist of the 1930s, displaying characteristics of the Bauhaus and Art Deco styles.